CHICKEN SOUP
A COLLECTION OF
YIDDISH SAYINGS

Great Quotations Publishing Company

Compiled by Peggy Schaffer
Cover Art by Kathy Davis
Cover Design by Jeff Maniglia
Typeset and Design by Caroline Solarski and Julie Otlewis

— —

© 1993 Great Quotations Publishing Company

Published in the United States by:
Great Quotations Publishing Company
1967 Quincy Court
Glendale Heights, IL 60139

Printed in Hong Kong

ISBN: 1-56245-069-7

For Mollie and Jack
with love and appreciation.

• • • •

To work for another man
is often like taking honey from a bee:
accompanied by a sting.

• • • •

■ ■ ■ ■

Worries go down better with soup
than without.

■ ■ ■ ■

• • • •

*This world can be changed
neither by cursing —
nor by laughing.*

• • • •

■ ■ ■ ■

If all men pulled in one direction,
the world would keel over.

■ ■ ■ ■

• • • •

So it goes in this world:
one man has the purse,
the other the money.

• • • •

■ ■ ■ ■

*T*he world is like a ladder:
one man goes up
while another goes down.

■ ■ ■ ■

• • • •

If I do not utter a word,
I am its master;
once I utter it, I am its slave.

• • • •

■ ■ ■ ■

It is better to be a footstool
to a king
than a king of fools.

■ ■ ■ ■

• • • •

Work is easy —
for those who like to work.

• • • •

■ ■ ■ ■

In a good apple,
you sometimes find a worm.

■ ■ ■ ■

• • • •

God did not create woman from man's head,
that he should command her;
nor from his feet,
that she should be his slave;
but from his side,
that she should be nearest his heart.

— adapted from The Talmud

• • • •

■　■　■　■

Culture in a woman
is worth more than gold.

■　■　■　■

• • • •

Don't deny a pregnant woman's wish.

• • • •

■ ■ ■ ■

A woman of sixty, like a girl of six,
will run at the sound of wedding music.

■ ■ ■ ■

• • • •

*T*he ideal man has a man's strength and
the compassion of a woman.

• • • •

■ ■ ■ ■

Be careful not to make women weep,
for God counts their tears.

— Talmud

■ ■ ■ ■

• • • •

If you eat your bagel,
you'll have nothing left but the hole.

• • • •

■ ■ ■ ■

Give your ear to all,
your hand to your friends,
but your lips only to your wife.

■ ■ ■ ■

• • • •

If each one sweeps before his own door,
the whole street will be clean.

• • • •

■ ■ ■ ■

Why is it that fools have pretty wives?

■ ■ ■ ■

• • • •

It does no harm
to listen to one's own wife.

• • • •

■ ■ ■ ■

If you love your wife,
you love her family, too.

■ ■ ■ ■

• • • •

Celebrations have to be made,
troubles come by themselves.

• • • •

■ ■ ■ ■

House and wealth are inherited
from our fathers;
but a sensible wife is a gift from the Lord.

— Book of Proverbs, 19:14

■ ■ ■ ■

• • • •

Wisdom is with aged men,
and understanding in length of days.

— Book of Job, 12:12

• • • •

■ ■ ■ ■

The man who thinks wisdom
is greater than virtue
will lose his wisdom.

■ ■ ■ ■

• • • •

*B*eing in the company of a wise man
is like going in to a perfumery;
you may buy nothing,
but the scent will cling to you
for a day.

• • • •

■ ■ ■ ■

Man is wise
only while searching for wisdom;
when he thinks he has found it,
he is a fool.

■ ■ ■ ■

• • • •

A wise man's question
contains half the answer.

• • • •

■　■　■　■

The wise are pleased
when they discover truths;
fools are pleased
when they discover falsehoods.

■　■　■　■

• • • •

A short life with wisdom is better than
a long life without it.

• • • •

■ ■ ■ ■

Wisdom is the light in man.

■ ■ ■ ■

• • • •

Wisdom, like wine,
keeps best in a plain vessel.

• • • •

■　■　■　■

Wealth brings anxiety,
but wisdom leads to peace of mind.

■　■　■　■

• • • •

The beginning of wisdom is to desire it.

• • • •

■ ■ ■ ■

We would all be rich —
if we didn't have to eat.

■ ■ ■ ■

• • • •

What good is a silver urn
if it is full of tears?

• • • •

■ ■ ■ ■

If you sit in a hot bath
you think the whole town is warm.

■ ■ ■ ■

. . . .

Who is really rich?
The man who is satisfied with his share.

. . . .

■ ■ ■ ■

The tongue is the most dangerous
of weapons.

■ ■ ■ ■

• • • •

Truth shows in the eyes;
lies stay behind the eyes.

• • • •

■ ■ ■ ■

*U*ltimately, truth rises,
like oil on water.

■ ■ ■ ■

• • • •

Half a truth is a whole lie.

■ ■ ■ ■

A lie one must not say;
and some truths you should not tell.

■ ■ ■ ■

• • • •

*B*etter the ugly truth than a beautiful lie.

• • • •

■ ■ ■ ■

No other purpose
should be attached to truth
than that you should know what is true.

■ ■ ■ ■

• • • •

A truth does not become greater
by repetition.

• • • •

■ ■ ■ ■

*Troubles that don't show on the face
lie on the heart.*

■ ■ ■ ■

• • • •

He who comes late
must eat what is left.

• • • •

■ ■ ■ ■

*T*roubles are as common as wood,
but they can't heat up the oven.

■ ■ ■ ■

• • • •

When you tell the truth
you don't have to remember what you said.

• • • •

■ ■ ■ ■

In seeking knowledge,
the first step is silence,
the second listening,
the third remembering,
the fourth practicing, and the fifth —
teaching others.

■ ■ ■ ■

• • • •

One mother can achieve more
than a hundred teachers.

• • • •

■ ■ ■ ■

When we laugh, everyone sees it;
when we weep, no one does.

■ ■ ■ ■

• • • •

What soap is for the body,
tears are for the soul.

• • • •

■ ■ ■ ■

Caution at first is better
than tears at last.

■ ■ ■ ■

• • • •

Ink dries fast;
tears do not.

• • • •

■ ■ ■ ■

The heart does not mean
everything the tongue utters.

■ ■ ■ ■

• • • •

Those who talk a lot
usually talk about themselves.

• • • •

■ ■ ■ ■

The tongue is more dangerous
than a dagger.

■ ■ ■ ■

• • • •

One word too many serves no purpose.

• • • •

■ ■ ■ ■

If you talk too much,
you'll say what you didn't want to.

■ ■ ■ ■

• • • •

Our eyes and ears
do not always depend upon our will power,
but a man's tongue does.

• • • •

■ ■ ■ ■

It is better to abstain from talking
than from eating.

■ ■ ■ ■

• • • •

You may regret your silence once,
but you will regret your talk twice.

• • • •

■ ■ ■ ■

The mouth is a door
and should be kept shut.

■ ■ ■ ■

• • • •

The suspense is often worse
than the ordeal.

• • • •

■ ■ ■ ■

*R*espect the stranger—
and remain suspicious.

■ ■ ■ ■

• • • •

Better one word in time
than two ill-timed.

• • • •

■ ■ ■ ■

The proud man thinks,
"Wherever I sit is the front."

■ ■ ■ ■

• • • •

The conceited man is not a sinner,
but a fool.

• • • •

■ ■ ■ ■

*Fools do not know
what a prison they live in.*

■ ■ ■ ■

• • • •

Prisoners are free
if content with their state;
free men who seek more then their lot
are prisoners to desire.

• • • •

■ ■ ■ ■

To be patient can be better
than being rich.

■ ■ ■ ■

• • • •

You can drain a whole brook,
or drill through the hardest granite,
if only you have enough patience.

• • • •

■ ■ ■ ■

Better a bad peace than a good war.

■ ■ ■ ■

• • • •

When you quarrel,
do it in such a way
that you can make up.

• • • •

■ ■ ■ ■

*T*hose who are ashamed of their parents
can win neither blessings nor praises.

■ ■ ■ ■

• • • •

Not teaching your children to work
is like teaching them to steal.

— Talmud

• • • •

■ ■ ■ ■

Let us be grateful to our parents:
had they not been tempted,
we would not be here.

— Talmud

■ ■ ■ ■

• • • •

Honor your father and mother,
even as you honor God;
for all three were partners
in your creation.

• • • •

■ ■ ■ ■

The man who disobeys his parents
will have disobedient sons.

■ ■ ■ ■

• • • •

The pot that belongs to partners
is neither hot nor cold.

• • • •

■ ■ ■ ■

God could not be everywhere,
so he created mothers.

■ ■ ■ ■

• • • •

A mother has glass eyes,
she cannot see her children's faults.

• • • •

■ ■ ■ ■

A mother understands
what a child does not say.

■ ■ ■ ■

• • • •

Mothers have big aprons —
to cover the faults of their children.

• • • •

■ ■ ■ ■

The mother-in-law and the daughter-in-law should not ride in the same cart.

■ ■ ■ ■

• • • •

Money really adds no more to the wise
than clothes can to the beautiful.

• • • •

■ ■ ■ ■

A purse without money
is only a piece of leather.

■ ■ ■ ■

• • • •

Money can buy anything —
except sense.

• • • •

■ ■ ■ ■

If you can't help out with a little money,
at least give a sympathetic groan.

■ ■ ■ ■

• • • •

A heavy purse is light to carry.

• • • •

■   ■   ■   ■

A third person may not interfere
between two
who sleep on the same pillow.

■   ■   ■   ■

• • • •

Some people are like new shoes:
the cheaper they are,
the louder they squeak.

• • • •

■ ■ ■ ■

Man comes into the world with an Oy!
and leaves with a Gevalt!

■ ■ ■ ■

• • • •

To love mankind is easy;
to love man is hard.

• • • •

■ ■ ■ ■

Man is endowed by nature with two eyes;
one to see his neighbors' virtues,
the other to see his own faults.

■ ■ ■ ■

• • • •

Liquor's tongue reveals what is on the mind.

• • • •

■ ■ ■ ■

To jump to a conclusion
is to by-pass the process of proof.

■ ■ ■ ■

• • • •

If you seek a faultless friend,
you will remain friendless.

• • • •

■ ■ ■ ■

A son in this world prevents loneliness
in the world to come.

■ ■ ■ ■

• • • •

*T*he man who thinks
he can live without others
is mistaken;
the man who thinks
others can't live without him
is more mistaken.

• • • •

■ ■ ■ ■

Love me a little less,
but longer.

■ ■ ■ ■

• • • •

To promise and to love cost no money.

• • • •

■ ■ ■ ■

Ever since dying came into fashion,
life hasn't been safe.

■ ■ ■ ■

• • • •

Life is the greatest of bargains:
we get it for nothing.

• • • •

In this life,
luck won't help you
unless you cooperate.

• • • •

What you fall into you can fall out of.

• • • •

■ ■ ■ ■

When life isn't the way you like,
like it the way it is.

■ ■ ■ ■

• • • •

Pray that you will never have to bear
all that you can endure.

• • • •

■　■　■　■

If you sing before you get out of bed,
you'll cry before you go to sleep.

■　■　■　■

• • • •

He who seeks to know everything
grows old quickly.

• • • •

■ ■ ■ ■

Learning is more important than action —
when it leads to action.

— Talmud

■ ■ ■ ■

• • • •

Much have I learned from my teachers,
more from my colleagues,
but most from my students.

— Talmud

• • • •

■ ■ ■ ■

Some men study so much
they don't have time to know.

■ ■ ■ ■

• • • •

*T*he head of a fool is like a broken dish:
it will not hold knowledge.

• • • •

■ ■ ■ ■

It is better to know nothing
than to learn nothing.

■ ■ ■ ■

• • • •

A light for one is a light for a hundred.

- Talmud

• • • •

■ ■ ■ ■

When wine comes in,
knowledge goes out.

■ ■ ■ ■

• • • •

Knowledge that is paid for
will be longer remembered.

• • • •

■ ■ ■ ■

*Jews are just like everyone else —
only more so.*

■ ■ ■ ■

• • • •

If a Jew breaks a leg,
he thanks God he did not break both legs;
if he breaks both legs,
he thanks God he did not break his neck.

• • • •

■ ■ ■ ■

The joy of Jews is never free of anxiety.

■ ■ ■ ■

• • • •

Silence is the only good substitute
for intelligence.

• • • •

■ ■ ■ ■

If you want to be considered smart,
just agree with everyone.

■ ■ ■ ■

•   •   •   •

*Honors are like a shadow;
the harder you chase them,
the further they run from you.*

•   •   •   •

■ ■ ■ ■

Honor is measured by the one who gives it,
not be the one who receives it.

■ ■ ■ ■

• • • •

It is better to die on your feet
than to live on your knees.

• • • •

■ ■ ■ ■

*T*he man who gives with a smile
is more honorable
than the man who gives with a wince.

■ ■ ■ ■

• • • •

No labor, however humble,
dishonors the man.

— Talmud

• • • •

■ ■ ■ ■

*T*he place does not honor the man;
the man honors the place.

— Talmud

■ ■ ■ ■

• • • •

As long as a man breathes
he should not lose hope.

— Talmud

• • • •

■ ■ ■ ■

Things can be good anywhere,
but they're even better at home.

■ ■ ■ ■

• • • •

A man who never leaves his home
is like a man who spends his life in prison.

• • • •

■ ■ ■ ■

The trip is never too hard,
if you know you're going home.

■ ■ ■ ■

• • • •

A man is not honest
just because he has had no chance to steal.

• • • •

■ ■ ■ ■

It is not the rich who pay;
it is the honest.

■ ■ ■ ■

• • • •

If you walk straight,
you won't fall.

• • • •

■ ■ ■ ■

When the heart is full,
it is the eyes that overflow.

■ ■ ■ ■

• • • •

A man's heart is a lock,
but even a lock can be opened
with the right key.

• • • •

■ ■ ■ ■

God looks at a man's heart
before he looks at a man's brains.

■ ■ ■ ■

• • • •

The heart of a man
and the bottom of the sea
are unfathomable.

• • • •

■ ■ ■ ■

When you pour your heart out,
it feels lighter.

■ ■ ■ ■

• • • •

*G*od knows that the best synagogue
is the human heart.

• • • •

■ ■ ■ ■

When a habit begins to cost money,
it's called a hobby.

■ ■ ■ ■

• • • •

*T*he most common habit is gossip —
and it causes the most trouble.

• • • •

■ ■ ■ ■

From happiness to sorrow
takes a moment;
from sorrow to happiness
takes years.

■ ■ ■ ■

• • • •

*T*he only thing speed is good for
is catching flies.

• • • •

■ ■ ■ ■

What you don't see with your eyes,
don't invent with your mouth.

■ ■ ■ ■

• • • •

One enemy is too many;
and a hundred friends are not enough.

• • • •

■ ■ ■ ■

A big blow from a stranger hurts less than a small blow from a friend.

■ ■ ■ ■

• • • •

We all remain better friends —
at a slight distance.

• • • •

■ ■ ■ ■

Your friend has a friend —
so tell him no secrets.

■ ■ ■ ■

• • • •

*T*hose who want to be forgiven
must learn to forgive.

• • • •

■ ■ ■ ■

If you take revenge, you will regret it;
if you forgive, you will rejoice.

■ ■ ■ ■

• • • •

A fool can ask more questions in an hour
than ten wise men can answer in a year.

• • • •

When a fool goes to market,
the merchants rejoice.

• • • •

Don't ask a fool a question —
or give him an explanation.

• • • •

■ ■ ■ ■

*Drunkards sober up,
but fools remain fools.*

■ ■ ■ ■

• • • •

If a fool says nothing,
you can't tell whether he's a fool or a sage.

• • • •

Borscht and bread make your cheeks red.

• • • •

All is not cream that comes from the cow.

• • • •

■ ■ ■ ■

*T*rue faith needs neither evidence
nor research.

■ ■ ■ ■

• • • •

No one can know how the shoe pinches
except the one who walks in it.

• • • •